Contents

Words printed in **bold** are explained in the glossary.

♡ Everybody's different

All of us are different. Look at your friends. Some are boys and some are girls. Some like playing sports, while others don't. Nobody is quite like you.

People with a **disability** cannot use a part of their body or their mind. This also makes them different.

However, we all have many things in common, too.

Some people with a physical disability find it hard to walk, so they use special wheelchairs, like this one.

Think of all the things that you have in common with your friends. Now think of the things that are different about you.

Having a disability does not mean you cannot do things. You just have to work harder to do some of the things that many people take for granted. The charities described in this book work to make life easier and more enjoyable for disabled people.

Charities are given money by the public to help people.

♥ The right help

Do you have a younger brother or sister? If so, you may remember how tiring babies can be. They need lots of love and attention. This can leave mums and dads and brothers and sisters feeling tired and unsure about how to best care for them.

When a baby is born with disabilities, these feelings are even stronger.

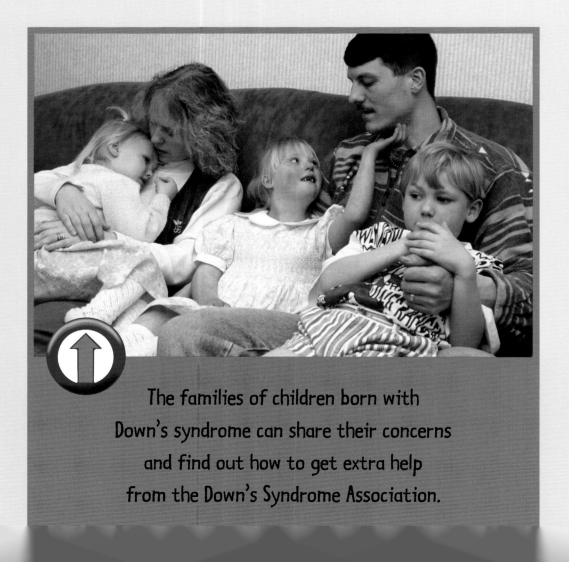

The families of children born with Down's syndrome can share their concerns and find out how to get extra help from the Down's Syndrome Association.

CASE STUDY

Alex (left) has **autism**. He finds it hard to understand and communicate with other people. The National Autistic Society has helped his family understand his difficulties. The society's Early Bird Programme has introduced them to ways which can help Alex fit in more happily with the family and with others. Alex and his family are now making great progress.

Learning and school

Do any of the children at your school have any disabilities? Probably. In the past, nearly all children with disabilities went to special schools. Now most disabled children go to their local school with their friends.

The Royal National Institute for the **Blind** (RNIB) provides special equipment for children who are blind or cannot see well, so they can do the same lessons as sighted children.

This tactile globe helps children who cannot see to find out about the Earth.

How would you get around your school if you could not see? What would you need to help you?

This special typewriter is for people who cannot see well. It makes bumps on the paper so that letters can be felt rather than seen.

John (4) cannot see. He finds it difficult to move and to learn. Someone from the charity KIDS visits him and his mum once a week. Together they help John relax and learn to enjoy playing with toys. He and his family are much happier now.

♥ Out and about

If you were in a wheelchair, would you be able to do all the things you do now? Could you get up kerbs, play games or go into shops?

The charity Whizz-Kidz provides electric wheelchairs that are specially made for each child. Rhys (5) has weak muscles, so he cannot walk. With his Whizz-Kidz wheelchair though, he can race his friends down the street and go wherever he likes.

Rhys's wheelchair moves up and down, and is easy to control.

The Guide Dogs for the Blind Association does many things to help people who cannot see well. It has trained Ghow to use a long cane to help him get around on his own. 'Anything that stops me having to rely on others has to be a good thing,' he says.

Ghow feels the ground in front of him with his cane, to find out what is there.

Ramps and wide doorways help people in wheelchairs. Can you think of other things that help disabled people get around?

♥ Having fun

What do you like doing in your spare time? Are there any sports and games you couldn't play if you were blind or **deaf** or had problems moving around?

With the proper equipment and support, people with disabilities can enjoy exciting sports, such as hang-gliding.

Steve has **cerebral palsy**, which makes it difficult for him to speak, walk and control his muscles. It doesn't stop him flying though. Eight years ago he set up the charity Flyability, giving people with disabilities the chance to enjoy hang-gliding and paragliding and to learn to become pilots.

These children are enjoying a Phab outing.

Phab is a charity which runs clubs across the UK for children, young people and adults. Some of the people have disabilities, others don't. Together they play sports and games, and share their interests.

Every year, charities arrange day trips and holidays for hundreds of people with disabilities.

This walking holiday was arranged by a charity to allow disabled people to get the most out of the countryside.

♡ Getting a job

What do you want to be when you grow up? If you have a disability you may find it harder to do what you want to do, as many businesses do not employ disabled people.

MENCAP helped Richard, who has **learning difficulties**, get a job at the library in the Houses of Parliament. They helped him learn how to do his job and still support him. Richard says, 'I work hard and have got to know people here. The bosses are brilliant.'

Seven years ago, Sarah was knocked off her bike when doing a paper round. She now needs to use a wheelchair. She decided she wanted to work with plants, so the Enham Trust provided her with with a home and taught her all about plants to help her find a job.

With help from the Enham Trust, Sarah is making the most of her life.

Extra help

Some people with disabilities may need extra help to do all the things they want to do.

Canine Partners for Independence (CPI) trains dogs to help people who can't walk or use their hands and arms properly. This means that the owners are able to look after themselves.

The CPI dogs can open and shut doors, switch lights on and off and even unload a washing machine.

CASE STUDY

It can be very tiring looking after someone every day, as you never get the chance to get out of the house. Crossroads Caring for Carers gives carers a break, so that they can go out sometimes. Dave's mum says, 'When our care worker walks through the door, it brings instant relief. We know that we are both in expert hands.'

♥ My own home

When you are older, you will probably want your own home. For disabled people, this is not always possible as many places are not suitable for people who find it hard to move around.

Scope provides housing that has been adapted for disabled people. And there is always a member of staff around to help sort out any problems.

The kitchens in the Scope houses have special low worktops, so that people in wheelchairs can reach them easily.

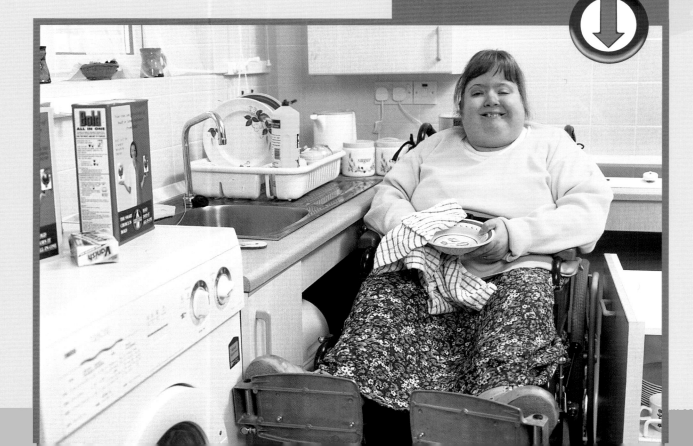

Daniel (11), Mark (10) and David (8) all have cerebral palsy, which makes it difficult for them to walk. The John Grooms Housing Association provided them with a home that has wide doorways, a lift and a shower that can be used by someone in a wheelchair.

The boys' mum, Dawn, says, 'The boys now go where they want, when they want. They do not need me or their dad to carry them.'

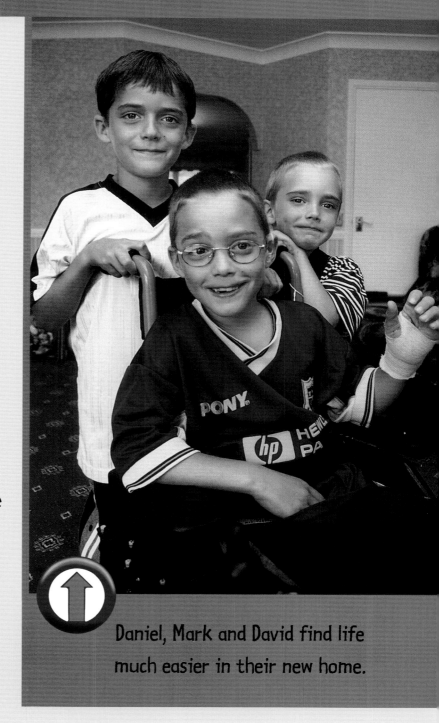

Daniel, Mark and David find life much easier in their new home.

Could someone in a wheelchair get into your home?

♥ Hobbies and interests

Do you like films or meeting up with your friends? Imagine that you wanted to go to the cinema but they wouldn't let you in as there was no space for a wheelchair. You'd be pretty fed up!

The charity, Artsline, lets disabled people know which theatres, cinemas and museums can be used by people who are blind, deaf or in wheelchairs.

Artsline also arranges dance, drama and art activities for people with disabilities.

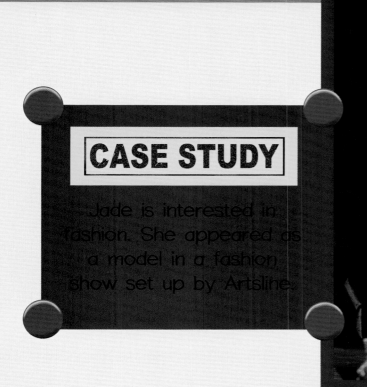

For those who like excitement, many charities now arrange trips to faraway countries. They give people the chance to visit new places and try new experiences.

The Guide Dogs for the Blind Association arranges fund-raising trips all over the world which include blind people.

♥ Medical research

Some people become disabled after an accident, others are born with a disability. Sometimes we know why people are born with a disability, but often there is no obvious reason why it has happened.

Every year charities spend millions of pounds trying to find out what has caused a disability and how it can be prevented in the future.

Sara has a kind of **muscular dystrophy** which makes her muscles very weak. She wears splints to support her legs and has to use a wheelchair to travel any distance.

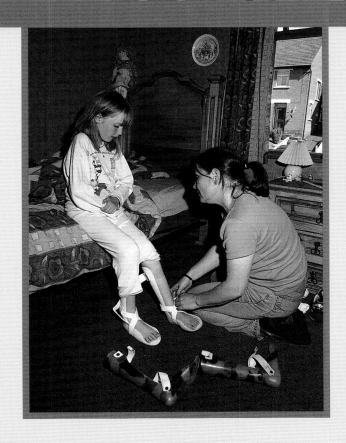

Sara's mum, Kathy, raises money for the Muscular Dystrophy Campaign so that doctors can learn more about what causes the condition and find a cure. 'I am sure that medical research will find an answer eventually,' she says.

Sara enjoys a shopping trip with her mum and her friend, Moya.

♡ Helping ourselves

Every day disabled people are told they can't do certain things, go to certain places, or be the same as everyone else – just because they have a disability.

How would that make you feel? You would probably be very angry and upset.

People with disabilities want to enjoy life as much as everyone else.

That is why more and more disabled people and their families are getting involved with charities.

Today, many people with disabilities work for charities as they know what help is needed most.

The Royal Association for Disability and Rehabilitation (RADAR) is a charity that is run by people with disabilities, and employs a number of staff who have disabilities. The charity campaigns for disabled people to be able to do the same things as people who don't have disabilities.

♡ Raising money

Charities are able to help others because they are given money to do so. This money is given by governments, businesses and people like you and me. Together we raise millions of pounds each year.

If you are trying to collect money for a good cause, a clever way to attract attention is by dressing up in funny costumes.

The easiest way to help charities is to put money in a collection box. But there are many more fun ways. It doesn't matter how silly or simple the idea is – as long as it helps. You could have a sponsored cake or toy sale, a bike ride or a sponsored silence at your school.

Every year, many cities around the world hold a very long race called a marathon. The London Marathon and the New York Marathon are two of the biggest events, with several thousand runners taking part. A lot of these runners are sponsored to raise money for many different charities.

This marathon runner is raising money for The Guide Dogs for the Blind Association.

How could you support a charity for people with disabilities?

♥ How you can help

Have you ever helped anyone? It can feel good to do something kind and generous. You can help by:

● contacting a charity that you are interested in (see pages 30-31) to find out more about what they do. Many charities have children's clubs that include competitions and games, as well as providing information.

● asking your teacher to get someone from a charity supporting a disabled group to come and talk to your class.

● treating all people with disability you meet with respect.

● raising some money for the disability charity of your choice on your own or through your school. Get your parent or carer or teacher to contact the charity to find out more.

# Glossary

autism a person with autism finds it difficult to understand what others are feeling or what they mean when they speak. The ability to learn and understand varies a great deal from one person with autism to another.

blind someone who can see very little or nothing at all.

cerebral palsy when a part of the brain is injured at birth, which makes it difficult for someone to use parts of their body. Many people with cerebral palsy have some form of learning difficulty, but others don't.

deaf someone who can hear very little or nothing at all.

disability when a part of your body or mind does not work as expected.

Down's syndrome a condition someone is born with. People with Down's syndrome find it harder to learn things. Someone with Down's syndrome may also have difficulty seeing or hearing.

learning difficulty when a part of someone's brain does not work as expected and it takes them longer to learn things. It doesn't mean they cannot learn at all, just that it takes longer.

muscular dystrophy the name given to a number of conditions that make people's muscles very weak. As a result, they may find it difficult to use their arms and legs and may need a wheelchair.

physical disability when someone cannot use a part of their body as expected. This includes people who are blind or deaf, as well as people who cannot use their arms or legs or hands or feet.

♥ Contact details

All the charities in this book do many more things to help people with disabilities than those described. Contact them to find out more.

Artsline
020 7388 2227
www.artsline.org.uk
access@artsline.org.uk

Crossroads - Caring for Carers
020 7380 1133
www.crossroads.org.uk

Down's Syndrome Association
020 8682 4001
www.dsa-uk.com
info@downs-syndrome.org.uk

Flyability
www.flyability.org.uk
contact@flyability.org.uk

John Grooms Housing Association
020 7452 2000
www.johngrooms.org.uk
charity@johngrooms.org.uk

Guide Dogs for the Blind Association
0870 600 2323
www.guidedogs.org.uk
guidedogs@guidedogs.org.uk

KIDS
020 7359 3635
www.kids-online.org.uk
nat.off@kids-online.org.uk

MENCAP
020 7454 0454
www.mencap.org.uk

Muscular Dystrophy Campaign
020 7720 8055
www.muscular-dystrophy.org
info@muscular-dystrophy.org

National Autistic Society
020 7833 2299
www.nas.org.uk
info@nas.org.uk

Phab
020 8667 9443
www.phabengland.org.uk
info@phabengland.org.uk

The Royal Association for Disability and
Rehabilitation (RADAR)
020 7250 3222
www.radar.org.uk
radar@radar.org.uk

Royal National Institute for the Blind [RNIB]
020 7388 1266
www.rnib.org.uk
helpline@rnib.org.uk

Scope
020 7619 7100
www.scope.org.uk
Helpline 0808 800 3333

Winged Fellowship Trust
020 7833 2594
www.wft.org.uk

Whizz-Kidz
020 7233 6600
www.whizz-kidz.org.uk
info@whizz-kidz.org.uk

Organisations in Australia and New Zealand

Disabled Children's Foundation Inc.
(08) 9201 1030
www.eaglemedia.com.au/
wcs/dcf

Australian Quadriplegic Association Ltd
(02) 9661 8855
www.spinalcordinjuries.com.au

Royal Institute for Deaf and Blind
Children
www.ridbc.org.au

Index